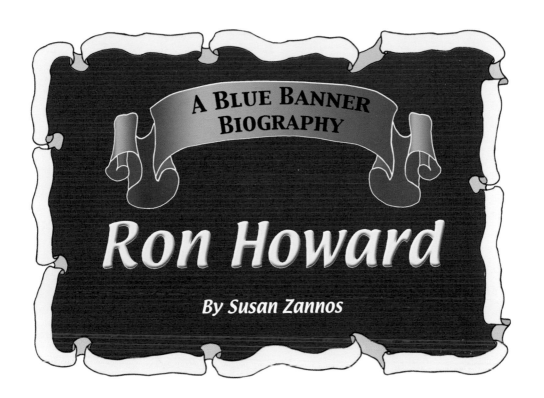

A BLUE BANNER
BIOGRAPHY

Ron Howard

By Susan Zannos

P.O. Box 619
Bear, Delaware 19701
Visit us on the web: www.mitchelllane.com
Comments? email us: mitchelllane@mitchelllane.com

Mitchell Lane
PUBLISHERS

Blue Banner Biographies

Sally Field	Jodie Foster	Melissa Gilbert
Rudy Giuliani	Ron Howard	Michael Jackson
Mary-Kate and Ashley Olsen	Shirley Temple	Richie Valens
Rita Williams-Garcia	Eminem	Daniel Radcliffe
Nelly		

Library of Congress Cataloging-in-Publication Data
Zannos, Susan.
    Ron Howard / Susan Zannos
        p. cm. — (A blue banner biography.)
    Includes index.
    Filmography: p.
    Summary: A biography of the actor, filmmaker, and director, Ron Howard.
    ISBN 1-58415-185-4 (library bound)
       1. Howard, Ron—Juvenile literature. 2. Motion picture producers and directors—United States—Biography—Juvenile literature. 3. Actors—United States—Biography—Juvenile literature. I. Title. II. Series.
PN1998.3.H689 Z36 2003
791. 43'0233'092--dc21
    [B]   2002014358

ABOUT THE AUTHOR: Susan Zannos has been a lifelong educator, having taught at all levels, from preschool to college, in Mexico, Greece, Italy, Russia, and Lithuania, as well as in the United States. She has published a mystery *Trust the Liar* (Walker and Co.) and *Human Types: Essence and the Enneagram* was published by Samuel Weiser in 1997. She has written several books for children, including *Chester Carlson and the Development of Xerography* and *Cesar Chavez* (Mitchell Lane). Susan lives in Oregon House, California.
PHOTO CREDITS: Cover: AP Photos; p. 4 Philip Caruso/Globe Photos; p. 8 John Barrett/Globe Photos; p. 10 TV Land; p. 13 AP Photos; p. 16 Globe Photos; p. 17 TV Land; p. 20 Bettmann/Corbis; p. 23 TV Land; p. 26 John Krondes/Globe Photos; p. 27 Globe Photos; p. 28 Alec Michael/Globe Photosp. 29 AP Photos.
ACKNOWLEDGMENTS: The following story has been thoroughly researched, and to the best of our knowledge, represents a true story. While every possible effort has been made to ensure accuracy, the publisher will not assume liability for damages caused by inaccuracies in the data, and makes no warranty on the accuracy of the information contained herein. This story has not been authorized nor endorsed by Ron Howard.

CONTENTS

Ron Howard has been in show business for so long, some people joke that he started months before he was born. He is one of the few child stars who has been able to work in show business all his life.

Playing the Game

Movie actor Tom Hanks worked with director Ron Howard in movies such as *Splash* and *Apollo 13*. In an interview for *People* magazine, Hanks said that Ron Howard "has seen absolutely everything that can possibly happen on a set, because the man started doing it three months before he was born or something like that." Of course that was a joke, but it was very close to the truth. In fact, some doctors think that unborn babies are able to hear what's going on around them, so it may have been the truth.

Rance Howard, Ron's father, was an actor, director, and writer. His mother, Jean Speegle Howard, was an actress. Before Ron was born he was in theaters where actors were rehearsing plays and performing them. When Ron arrived in his parents' hometown of Duncan, Oklahoma, on March 1, 1954, his father was touring with a production of *Mr. Roberts* starring Henry Fonda. As little Ronny learned how to talk, he learned some of the lines spoken by Ensign Pulver in the play. His father played the part of Mr. Roberts. Baby Ronny thought it was a game he and his father played.

In an interview for *Seventeen* magazine, Ron Howard said that when he started acting with other people, "it was just a matter of playing the game with them, something I did for fun." He started playing the game when he was only eighteen months old. In 1956 the little Howard family—dad Rance, mom Jean, and Ronny—all appeared in the western movie *Frontier Woman*. When Ronny was two years old he was on stage in a production of *The Seven Year Itch*, which his father directed for the Hilltop Theater in Baltimore.

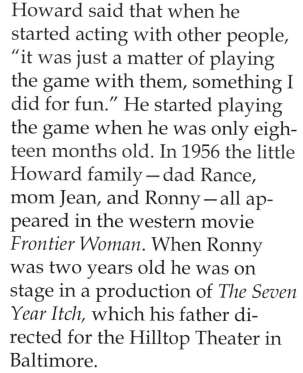

"It was just a matter of playing the game with them, something I did for fun," Ron Howard told Seventeen magazine.

Acting, and the world of moviemaking and television, never seemed strange to Ronny Howard. For him the actors and directors and cameramen were just ordinary people that he saw every day. When Ronny was four years old, Rance Howard was in New York talking to a casting director about an acting job. "He happened to be looking for a child for a film called

The Journey," Rance told an interviewer for *TV Guide*. "I told him I had a son. The next day I brought Ronny in, and that was that." The Howard family flew to Vienna, Austria, where the movie was made on location.

When they got back to the United States, Rance Howard decided to move to California. It was hard moving around and touring as an actor and director when he had a family. He thought he would have plenty of work in Hollywood without having to travel, and he was right. The Howards moved into a house in Burbank. Ronny's little brother, Clint, was born there on April 20, 1959.

Rance Howard did get a lot of acting jobs in Hollywood, but not big starring roles. He was also a writer and director, a well-known and respected professional. Ronny got a lot of jobs, too. He appeared in television plays on *Playhouse 90* and *General Electric Theatre*. "In those days," Rance Howard explained for *TV Guide*, "TV was still live." This meant that instead of being videotaped, the shows were broadcast as they were being acted. "The town was so awed by a five-year-old who could be depended upon not to fall apart in mid-scene that he did twenty-five shows in a row," his dad said.

"The town was so awed by a five-year-old who could be depended upon not to fall apart in mid-scene..." his dad said.

At the age when most little boys are just beginning kindergarten, Ronny Howard was already a professional television actor. He memorized his lines perfectly. He didn't think it was work. It was his favorite game and he loved to play it. A successful television producer, Sheldon Leonard, saw Ronny Howard perform on *General Electric Theatre*. Mr. Leonard was looking for a young boy to play the part of the sheriff's son on *The Andy Griffith Show*. He thought Ronny would be perfect for the part, and he was right. The part that Ronny Howard played, Opie Taylor, was a favorite with the television audiences. The series ran for eight years. Soon Ronny was getting parts in movies, too. In 1962 he had an important role in *The Music Man,* and in 1963 he played Eddie in *The Courtship of Eddie's Father.*

Rance Howard (right) with son, Ron.

Opie

*T*he *Andy Griffith Show* began in October 1960 and continued for eight years. It was in the top ten television shows the entire time. Andy Griffith was a popular film and television actor. He played the part of Andy Taylor, sheriff of Mayberry, North Carolina. Ronny Howard was his son, Opie. There was a strong supporting cast, including Don Knotts as deputy Barney Fife and Frances Bavier as Aunt Bee, who took care of Opie.

The opening camera shot at the beginning of the show is of the sheriff and his son going fishing, walking along and throwing a stone into the pond. "What I really remember," Ron Howard told interviewer Jim Axelrod for CBS News, "is that we only had three opportunities to throw that rock into the lake because it's one of the water reservoirs for Los Angeles. And we were allowed to throw only three rocks in there."

Rance and Jean Howard thought very seriously about their son Ronny being an actor. They knew that he loved acting and was very talented. But they also wanted him to have a normal childhood. Since they were both actors themselves, they knew that it wasn't easy for the two things to go together. They told Ronny that any time he didn't want to act anymore, he could quit. "I always felt loved," Ron Howard remembered in the interview with Axelrod. "I never felt that my parents' love or affection depended in any way, shape, or form on how I was doing at the set."

This is a classic scene from The Andy Griffith Show *where Andy, who played Sheriff Taylor, takes his son Opie (played by Ron Howard) fishing.*

Rance Howard always went with Ronny to the set of *The Andy Griffith Show*. On Thursdays when the writers, director, and cast members met for script readings, Rance read Opie's part because at the beginning Ronny didn't know how to read. Rance also helped his son learn his lines. One time when Ronny misbehaved, his father picked him up and spanked him. Ron told an interviewer for *Seventeen* magazine years later, "He explained that I had to be responsible, that people were trying to work." Rance made Ronny understand that if he wanted to act, he had to be professional.

On the other hand, Rance also protected his son. He spoke to the members of the cast and crew and told them not to tease Ronny or play around with him on the set. He explained that it was difficult for a child to know when it was appropriate to play and when it wasn't. Ronny's parents insisted that his contract have a special clause that said he did not have to make publicity appearances. They wanted him to have a normal life at home and in his school and neighborhood.

Rance read Opie's part because at the beginning Ronnie didn't know how to read. Rance also helped his son learn his lines.

"If I were to sit down and sort of write a list of my childhood highlights," Ron Howard told CBS News, "most of them would be the kid stuff . . . handling my-self against the school bully or something in the third grade, or it would be doing well in sports, or, you know, playing army with the kids on the block, and I lived on a block. I had all that." He was a good athlete and loved playing baseball. He was on a Little League team and never missed a game. During Little League season, the director had to ar-range the shooting schedule around Ronny's games.

> *Ron had a good relationship with Andy Griffith, who was like an uncle to him.*

The relationship between Sheriff Taylor and Opie was modeled on the real-life relation-ship between Rance Howard and Ronny. The boy also had a good relationship with Andy Griffith, who was like an uncle to him. His mother, Jean, frequently came to the set with his little brother, Clint, so that the whole family could have lunch together. As the years passed, Clint sometimes was on the show, too. He had the part of Leon, a little boy who always wore a cowboy suit.

Since Rance Howard was a writer, he sometimes wrote epi-sodes for *The Andy Griffith Show.* One of Ronny's favorites was a show his dad wrote that was based on a real experience. Once when Rance was umpire of his son's ball game, he called Ronny out at home base. Ronny and the other boys on his team thought he was safe, so there was an argument. Rance wrote a script about the incident, with Sheriff Taylor umpiring Opie's game. Ronny liked that show because it was a real experience — and because he got to play baseball at work.

Ron Howard was a popular child star who was much in demand because he could be counted on to act like a professional actor at a young age. This photo shows young Ron with co-stars Don Knotts (left) and Andy Griffith (right).

All-American Boy

Ronny Howard was a typical boy both on screen and off. While many child stars had a lot of problems when they started to grow up, Ronny didn't. One reason for this was that when he wasn't working, he went to public schools like most other children his age.

"In school I was always a novelty at first," he told interviewer Edwin Miller. "People got very jazzed up about the idea of having a kid actor in class. That would blow over in a couple of weeks, and then I was able to blend right in." When he was going to Burroughs High School in Burbank, he was on the basketball team. He didn't want to miss any of the practices or games. He didn't accept any acting jobs at all for nine months. "That's when I learned I missed acting," he said.

Another reason that Ronny Howard didn't have problems was that he really knew how to act. Many child stars know how to play only one role. When they get too old for that role, they don't know how to do anything else. But Ronny, and Clint, too, were actors who could play many different parts.

When *The Andy Griffith Show* ended in 1968, Ronny was fourteen years old. He was too old for little kid parts, but he continued to do guest appearances in television shows like *Gunsmoke* and *Lassie*. In 1971 he and his brother Clint began another television series, this one with famous actor Henry Fonda in *The Smith Family*. (Before that, Clint had starred in the film *Gentle Ben* about a boy with a pet bear. That led to the television series *Gentle Ben,* in which Clint also starred.) Also in 1971, Ronny and Clint starred together as members of a pioneer family in the movie *The Wild Country*. Rance Howard had a part in that movie, too.

Ron Howard graduated from Burroughs High School in 1972. He already knew what he wanted to do. On movie sets he had observed that it was the director who was in charge, who made things happen. That was what he wanted to do. He had an eight-millimeter camera. "By the time I was sixteen," he remembered in a *Los Angeles*

> **When *The Andy Griffith Show* ended in 1968, Ronny was fourteen years old. He was too old for little kid parts...**

Times article, "I was obsessed. I'd bully my little brother and his friends to be in all my movies." One of his films won an award in a national Kodak film contest.

By the time he graduated from high school, he also knew who he wanted to marry. During his junior year he fell in love with the redhead who sat in front of him in English class, Cheryl Alley. His parents tried to convince him that he and Cheryl were too young to get serious. But they were already serious.

After he graduated from high school, Ron enrolled in a film program at the University of Southern California. He also began working with director George Lucas

By the time he finished high school, Ron knew exactly who he would marry. Cheryl Alley was a redhead in his English class. A few years after graduation, Ron and Cheryl were married.

on the film *American Graffiti*. That movie was about one night in the lives of some boys who had just graduated from high school. Ron was the best-known actor in the film, but two of the others, Richard Dreyfuss and Harrison Ford, would go on to become famous actors. *American Graffiti* was a big success. It received five Academy Award nominations. While he was making that movie, Ron spent a lot of time learning about film-making from George Lucas.

As often happens when a movie is a big success, television executives decided to do a television series based on it. The series was called *Happy Days*. Ron

Ron (right) with director George Lucas. Ron first worked with Lucas during the filming of American Graffiti.

Howard starred in it as Richie Cunningham, a high school junior during the 1950s. The series was a hit. A reviewer for the *Washington Post* wrote: "*Happy Days* will be around for a while and the biggest reason . . . is the skill of the oldest young professional performer in television, Ron Howard."

Ron didn't have much time for his college courses. He left USC after four semesters. He thought that he could learn about directing while he was actually making movies. On June 7, 1975, a year after he started the series *Happy Days,* Ron and his high school sweetheart Cheryl got married. She was a student at Cal State at Northridge, where she earned a degree in psychology. They decided to wait to have children until Ron was finished with *Happy Days.*

"Happy Days will be around for a while and the biggest reason is the skill of the oldest young professional performer in television, Ron Howard."

The Big Chance

By the third year of the series *Happy Days*, the character Fonzie became a bigger hit with television audiences than Richie Cunningham. Fonzie was played by Henry Winkler. The show's ratings got better and better, and the television executives decided to make Winkler's part bigger. At first this made Ron Howard feel awkward, but fortunately he and Henry Winkler were friends, so it wasn't a big problem. Besides, when a show is a big success, it is good for everyone in the cast.

What was a problem for Ron were the publicity appearances he had to make. Now that he was an adult, he no longer had a clause in his contracts that said he didn't have to make appearances. He didn't like publicity tours. Thousands of fans would come to see the actors from *Happy Days.* Ron had always been shy, and he didn't like being mobbed by fans.

Ron kept thinking about being a director. If he could direct instead of act, he would still be working in a business he loved, but his appearance wouldn't be so well known. He talked to Cheryl about it. She agreed that he should try it. Pretty soon he got a chance. There was a producer, Roger Corman, who wanted Ron to star in a low-budget action movie. Ron didn't like the script, which was about car chases and crashes. But he knew that Corman was a producer who sometimes took a chance on new directors.

The character of Fonzie, played by Henry Winkler, right, soon became a hit with Happy Days' *audiences.*

Ron made a deal that he would star in the movie, which was called *Eat My Dust!*, if Corman would give him a chance to direct a movie. On his side, Corman made very clear that the movie Ron would direct also had to be a car chase movie, and that Ron would have to star in it besides directing it. The title of that movie was *Grand Theft Auto*. It was not the kind of movie Ron wanted to make, but he knew that he had to take advantage of the opportunity.

The whole family worked on the movie. Ron and Rance wrote the screenplay. Rance and Clint had parts in the movie. Cheryl began cooking for the crew, which had eighty-five members, because they were all tired of eating fast food. Ron managed to shoot the movie for a cost of $602,000. It grossed $15 million at the box office.

Ron kept thinking about being a director. Pretty soon he got a chance.

Ron still had two years on his contract for *Happy Days*. Roger Corman wanted him to do another film for him. But Ron had something else in mind. He had an agreement with NBC to direct a television movie. The story was one that Ron had been thinking about. He and his brother Clint worked on the script together. Because Ron was busy with *Happy Days,* Clint did most of the writing, and then the two of them would meet to go over the scenes.

They shot the television movie *Cotton Candy* on location at a high school in Dallas, Texas. Ron's mother, Jean, played the part of the teacher. His dad was the school's vice principal. Clint played one of the teenagers, and Ron's wife, Cheryl, played Clint's prom date.

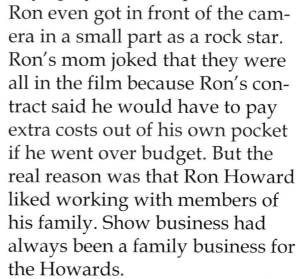

Ron Howard liked working with members of his family. Show business had always been a family business for the Howards.

Ron even got in front of the camera in a small part as a rock star. Ron's mom joked that they were all in the film because Ron's contract said he would have to pay extra costs out of his own pocket if he went over budget. But the real reason was that Ron Howard liked working with members of his family. Show business had always been a family business for the Howards.

In an Internet interview, Clint Howard talked about their childhood training. Clint is an actor with over a hundred film credits, and he received a lifetime achievement award in the 1998 MTV Movie Awards. Talking about their father, Clint said, "He explained to both Ron and me that it was a job, that being recognized by the public is part of it, that fame is false. . . . Your part is to go in, be prepared, and go in and act. And he gave us those simple fundamentals of the business. . . . I make the analogy that I was raised much like a kid in the circus is raised. Like that kid walking the high wire might seem spectacular to the audience below, but if that kid is learning how to walk that high wire when he's learning how to walk, then it's just going to come naturally . . . it was always fun. My dad always insisted, the one thing he insisted on was that we would prepare. And really, when you're prepared, that work is pretty much done."

Scenes from Happy Days *— Upper left: Ron Howard as Ritchie Cunningham, Henry Winkler as Arthur "Fonzie" Fonzarelli, and Anson Williams as "Potsie." Upper right: Ritchie and Potsie. Bottom: Tom Bosley as Howard Cunningham, Ritchie's dad with Ron Howard.*

Director

When Ron Howard's contract to play Richie Cunningham in the television series *Happy Days* expired in 1980, he left the show. *Happy Days* continued for four more years without him. Howard was ready to take his chances as a director. He and Cheryl were also ready to start their family. Their first daughter, Bryce, was born in 1981.

One problem that Ron Howard had at first as a director was that people had a hard time getting past the image of the characters he had played. How could anyone believe that Opie or Richie could be a film director? Everyone thought Ron Howard was too nice a guy to make the hard decisions a director had to make. When young producer Brian Grazer had an idea for a comedy, a movie about a mermaid, Ron wasn't sure he wanted to do it. They had trouble finding a studio to finance the movie. Walt Disney Studios was interested, but Ron hesitated. He thought it sounded too cute. "It seemed just too perfect," he said in an interview for *People* magazine. "Little Ronny Howard grows up to make films for Walt Disney Studios. That bothered me."

But Ron did direct it. It was *Splash,* his first big success as a director. It was also the first big success for the young actor who had the lead role, Tom Hanks. And as usual, Ron's father and brother and wife also had roles in the film. Ron Howard recalled in an interview for CBS News, "When we went and saw lines around the block for our movie, with no stars in it . . . That was just, you know, a sort of underdog sort of picture. It was one of the thrills of my professional life." As the film critic for *Newsweek* wrote, "After *Splash,* anyone who smirks at the notion that little Opie is a filmmaker is going to look like a fool."

"After Splash, anyone who smirks at the notion that little Opie is a filmmaker is going to look like a fool."

Ron Howard followed the mermaid movie with two other fantasies, *Cocoon,* a successful science fiction movie, and *Willow,* a big-budget fantasy film that was not a success. Another comedy, *Parenthood,* got good reviews. Ron Howard had quite a bit of experience with parenthood by then because his twin daughters, Jocelyn and Paige, had been born in 1985. In 1986 Ron and Cheryl moved to Connecticut so that their kids could grow up away from Hollywood. Even though Ron had a good experience as a child star, he didn't want that for his own children. One reason was because he knew he wouldn't have the time to spend on their careers the way his father had helped him with his. Ron's son Reed was born in 1987.

Meanwhile, Ron Howard and Brian Grazer became partners in Imagine Films Entertainment so that they could make the films they wanted to. In the early 1990s,

Ron with son Reed in 2002.

two action films, *Backdraft* (1991), about firefighters, and *Far and Away* (1992), about the Oklahoma land rush that Howard's ancestors had participated in, had only moderate success. Then in 1995 Howard demonstrated that he could create serious suspense. *Apollo 13*, the story of the failed moon mission, combined special effects, science, and suspense and was nominated for nine Oscars. (It won two, for Best Sound and Best Editing.) The Directors Guild of America gave Ron Howard their Outstanding Feature Film Directorial Achievement Award for *Apollo 13*. And once again the big breakthrough

Ron poses in his Beverly Hills office.

movie for Howard starred Tom Hanks, who was by then an important star.

Finally, in 2001, Ron Howard directed the film for which he was awarded an Oscar, the Academy Award for Best Director. The film was *A Beautiful Mind.* Actor Russell Crowe played the part of a mathematician who overcame the serious mental disease schizophrenia and later won a Nobel Prize. According to an interview in *Entertainment Weekly,* the idea for Howard's film about mental illness came from his days as Opie on *The Andy Griffith Show.*

Ron and Cheryl attended the Screen Actor's Guild Awards at Shrine Auditorium, 2002.

"There was an actor who was a guest," remembered Howard. "I was probably eight years old, but I could tell that this guy had been behaving strangely all day. And then he had this long scene, a big close-up. He started fine, but suddenly he was changing the dia-logue and disinte-

Ron and Brian Grazer are partners in Imagine Films Entertainment. Together they made A Beautiful Mind *for which Ron Howard was awarded an Oscar.*

grating into a monologue that turned into this self-loathing rant with him sobbing on the floor. Nobody knew what to do. . . . I remember looking at the director and he was stunned."

When Ron Howard thanked the members of his family in the speech accepting his Oscar, it wasn't just empty words. He said, "I'm grateful that I was raised by an extraordinary man, my father Rance Howard." And he talked about the support he had gotten from his mother, Jean Howard, who had died eighteen months before the awards ceremony. From the role of little Opie to the winner of the Academy Award for Best Director, Ron Howard had one success after another, largely because he didn't do it alone. It was a family business all the way.

CHRONOLOGY

1954	Born in Duncan, Oklahoma, on March 1
1956	Appears in film in *Frontier Woman* and on stage in *The Seven Year Itch*
1959	Travels to Vienna, Austria, with his family to make film *The Journey*; Howard family moves to Burbank, California; brother, Clint, is born
1960	Appears as Opie on *The Andy Griffith Show*, which runs for eight years
1962	Appears in film *The Music Man*
1963	Has role of Eddie in the film *The Courtship of Eddie's Father*
1971	Appears with Henry Fonda in *The Smith Family*
1972	Graduates from Burroughs High School in Burbank and enrolls in cinema studies at University of Southern California
1973	Stars in film *American Graffiti*
1974	Begins television series *Happy Days*, in which he stars for six years
1975	Marries his high school girlfriend, Cheryl Alley
1976	Stars in films *Eat My Dust* and *The Shootist* with John Wayne
1977	Directs, cowrites, and stars in the film *Grand Theft Auto*
1981	Daughter Bryce is born
1984	Directs first successful comedy, *Splash,* starring Tom Hanks
1985	Directs science fiction film, *Cocoon*; twin daughters, Jocelyn and Paige, are born
1986	Appears as Opie Taylor in television movie *Return to Mayberry*; moves his family to Connecticut; founds Imagine Films Entertainment with partner Brian Grazer
1987	Son Reed is born
1988	Directs big-budget fantasy film *Willow*
1989	Cowrites and directs successful comedy, *Parenthood*
1991	Directs *Backdraft*
1992	Directs *Far and Away*
1994	Directs *The Paper*
1995	Directs *Apollo 13,* for which he receives the Outstanding Feature Film Directorial Achievement Award from the Directors Guild of America
1996	Directs *Ransom*
1999	Directs *Edtv*
2000	Directs *How the Grinch Stole Christmas*; mother, Jean Howard, dies
2002	Receives Academy Award for Best Director for *A Beautiful Mind*
2003	Bronze statue of Andy Taylor and Opie installed at Pullen Park in Raleigh, NC

1956	*Frontier Woman:* acting
1959	*The Journey:* acting
1960–68	*The Andy Griffith Show,* television series: acting
1962	*The Music Man:* acting
1963	*The Courtship of Eddie's Father:* acting
1971	*The Smith Family,* television series: acting
1973	*American Graffiti:* acting
1974–80	*Happy Days,* television series: acting
1974	*The Spikes Gang:* acting
1976	*The Shootist:* acting
1976	*Eat My Dust!:* acting
1977	*Grand Theft Auto:* writing, directing, acting
1978	*Cotton Candy,* television movie: directing
1979	*More American Graffiti:* acting
1982	*Night Shift:* directing
1984	*Splash:* directing
1985	*Cocoon:* directing
1986	*Return to Mayberry,* television movie: acting
1986	*Gung Ho:* directing, producing
1988	*Willow:* directing
1989	*Parenthood:* writing, directing
1991	*Backdraft:* directing
1992	*Far and Away:* writing, directing, producing
1994	*The Paper:* directing
1995	*Apollo 13:* directing
1996	*Ransom:* directing
1999	*Edtv:* directing, producing
2000	*How the Grinch Stole Christmas:* directing, producing
2001	*A Beautiful Mind:* directing, producing
2003	*8 Mile:* producing

FOR FURTHER READING

Kramer, Barbara. *Ron Howard: Child Star and Hollywood Director.* Berkeley Heights, N.J.: Enslow Publishers, Inc., 1998.
Marcovitz, Hal. *Ron Howard.* Philadelphia: Chelsea House, 2002.

On theWeb:
BBC News | FILM | "Ron Howard's Happy Days" | January 23, 2002
news.bbc.co.uk/hi/English/entertainment/film/newsid_1777000/1777174.stm
CBS Sunday Morning | "Ron Howard: Too Good To Be True" | March 8, 2002
www.cbsnews.com/stories/2002/03/01/sunday/main502650.shtml
Ron Howard, Biography
www.hollywood.com/celebs/bio/celeb/1676876
74th Annual Academy Awards
www.oscar.com/oscarnight/winners/winner_directing.html

INDEX